W9-CQN-566

_DO_ grab + go bag _DO_
prep to evacuate

→ preplan for pets

→ predetermined meeting
place

The Homeowner's Guide
to Wildfire Prevention

→ prepare for 5-7 days

Are you Ready? Book by
FEMA

The Homeowner's Guide to Wildfire Prevention

Robert Sieben

Bay Tree Publishing, LLC, Point Richmond, California

© 2014 Robert Sieben

Feedback and comments are welcome at:
www.facebook.com/pages/Homeowner-Wildfire-Prevention/1595476730676861

Cover photo:

This photograph was taken by my wife at 11:30 A.M. on June 12, 2008, when a fire started by a cigarette on Tunnel Road threatened homes at Hiller Highlands on the top of the hill. Firefighters were able to take advantage of defensible space created by the removal of massive stands of French broom and Monterey pine seedlings to suppress the fire within a few hours.

Contents

Acknowledgements

The material found in this book is a compilation of several thousands of hours of hands on experience managing the wildlands between Hiller Highlands and Tunnel Road above Highway 24 since 1998. It also reflects knowledge gained from a variety of sources including presentations and discussions at meetings of the Oakland Wildfire Prevention Assessment District, the Diablo Firesafe Council, the Claremont Conservancy, and the presenters at the national Wildland Urban Interface Council.

I am especially indebted to the North Hills Community Association (NHCA) for sponsoring a series of workshops to develop these guidelines. Participants included former Assistant Fire Marshal Leroy Griffin; former Inspections Supervisor Camille Rodgers of the Oakland Fire Department; former Assistant Fire Chief of the EBRPD (East Bay Regional Park District) John Swanson; Cheryl Miller, a registered landscape architect and executive director of the Diablo Fire Safe Council; Carol Rice, a wildfire ecologist with Wildland Resource Management, Inc.; William McClung, my early mentor and a founder of the Claremont Conservancy; and members of the NHCA who asked the hard questions at the workshops.

In addition, I am deeply grateful to successive Boards of Directors of Phase V of Hiller Highlands, who over the past several years have budgeted from $7,000 to $12,000 annually for fire prevention; to the many volunteers from all phases of Hiller Highlands and other neighbors who have helped with our efforts; to the Diablo Fire Safe Council for four grants for fire prevention in the Hiller Highlands area, and to the Oakland WPAD and former City

Council members Jane Brunner and Henry Chang for providing free removal services for cut vegetation on several occasions.

Special thanks to the many citizen volunteers who have served so well on the Advisory Committee to the WPAD over the last ten years. Thanks as well to: the property owners in the Oakland hills who have voted to tax themselves to provide stable, dedicated funding of the WPAD; the City Council who voted to establish such a District; the dedicated staff of the OFD who worked to improve wildfire prevention in the Oakland hills; the EBRPD for providing monthly meeting facilities at no cost; the many guest experts who have spoken at meetings; Jerry Kent, former assistant general manager of operations of the EBRPD who oversaw its vegetation management program; and, posthumously, John Eliff, Batallion Chief of the CDF (California Department of Forestry), who was on site during the 1991 firestorm and was my early mentor.
—Robert Sieben

Introduction

There are a lot of things homeowners can and must do to prevent major wildfires from consuming their homes. These things have to be done before a firestorm hits and overwhelms firefighters, because once in motion such fires can be stopped only when the wind changes.

When firefighters are called upon to put out fires in the wildland-urban interface, they spend 70 percent of their time doing what property owners should have already done. *The Homeowner's Guide to Wildfire Prevention* provides the information homeowners need to take responsibility for making their property defensible, thereby increasing the chances their homes will survive a fire.

This guide is written by an Oakland hills homeowner who lives in a very high fire danger zone characterized by an intermix of wildlands and homes. He recognized that other fire prevention guides were of limited use since they were written for homes built on flat properties at a significant distance from their neighbors. In contrast, the Oakland Hills are characterized by steep, densely populated areas along narrow, winding streets, where residents live in close proximity to their neighbors or even share a pod with them. Such conditions are found in many of the coastal areas of California.

Unfortunately, most homeowners have no idea what they can do to avoid losing their homes and perhaps their lives to wildfire. The information in this guide can improve your chances of surviving an extreme wildfire. Most important, it describes the steps you need to take now, before a fire is approaching and it is too late.

Fire insurance may pay for some of your material losses in

a wildfire, but it will not replace the time, anguish, treasured personal items, and pets, nor will it restore the community lost in such a fire. Appropriate precautions can prevent your home from catching fire in the first place. While it doesn't replace fire insurance, it is both cheaper and more effective.

The guidelines in this book were developed by Robert Sieben, M.D., a resident of Hiller Highlands Homeowners Association, Phase V (HHV), consisting of 100 townhouses centered along Starview Drive and contiguous streets, including 14 acres of steep hillside property on the north side of Highway 24 just west of the Caldecott Tunnel in the Oakland hills. The catastrophic firestorm of 1991 began just northeast of this area and consumed the former residences within 20 minutes as ferocious northeasterly Diablo winds rapidly spread the devastating conflagration to areas throughout the nearby hills and across two major highways.

Dr. Sieben has been the volunteer coordinator of fire prevention for HHV since 1998. He is a physician with no prior experience in fire prevention who built a townhouse in the area after the firestorm. These guidelines represent what he has learned from thousands of hours of hands-on experience managing fire-prone vegetation on the large undeveloped portion of the homeowner association property. He served four terms on the Advisory Committee of the Oakland Wildfire Prevention Assessment District (WPAD), which he chaired, and also served on the North Hills Community Association, chairing its fire prevention committee. He has attended meetings of the Diablo Fire Safe Council and the National Wildlands Interface Council.

The pragmatic guidelines that follow are specific to the characteristics of the most dangerous, persistent, and difficult to manage fire hazards homeowners are likely to encounter in the Oakland hills. Since the options and techniques available to private property owners vary some from those available to the City of Oakland, these guidelines can not be officially endorsed by either the City or the committees on which Dr. Sieben has served. Nevertheless, they represent options for homeowners to consider on their own property.

At HHV the primary fire prevention strategy has evolved from an all-volunteer program to voluntary contributions to annual funding by the HHV Board of Directors, now at $70 per homeowner for a total of $7,000. The primary work is now done by Shelterbelt Builders Inc., an open land management and restoration company, and occasional volunteers under the supervision of Dr. Sieben.

The actual physical work requires an intimate knowledge both of the vegetation present and the appropriate management techniques required, plus the physical capacity to work on steep, hazardous terrain. While the land in question is unsuitable for goats, herbicides have been used selectively, sparingly, and in accordance with local laws without any ill effects.

As planting is difficult to sustain, HHV's approach has been to get rid of the bad stuff and let the good stuff grow, resulting in an improved natural landscape that is decidedly more fire safe without contributing to erosion or landslides. Although the bias has been toward encouraging native plants, many natives have been found to be of high fire risk—e.g., *Ceanothus*, elderberry, and coyote bush. When planting, direction and degree of slope, soil composition, exposure to Diablo winds, accessibility, density, and maintenance, all have to be taken into consideration.

The Oakland hills are representative of a Mediterranean climate, characterized by a rainy season from November to

April followed by a prolonged dry season from June to November. This climate is seen throughout the central valley and coastal hills of California.

Burning of brush is not feasible in this windy, densely inhabited corridor, so cuttings have been left in decomposition piles where appropriate, reducing the high cost of removal. The winter rainy season and lack of freezing temperatures or snow facilitate decomposition of the cut grasses, brush and trees.

This potential ignition site along Tunnel Road was cleared of dense brush and the trees were laddered. A fire safe zone was extended 200 feet up the slope to create a buffer zone around an inaccessible 60 degree slope and to protect a pair of thriving redwood groves.

Fire Prevention Tip #1:
Reduce the Sources of Ignition

Most fires in the Bay Area are caused by humans, not lightning. So, the first line of defense is to avoid starting a fire yourself. You need to be aware of the common sources of ignition and take precautions to control them, beginning within your home and then outside it and along the roadside.

Within Your Home

A major earthquake is expected to occur on the nearby Hayward fault at some time in the next several years. When, not if, this earthquake occurs, your home is far more likely to be destroyed by fire than by the earthquake itself. You can reduce this possibility by having a plumber install an automatic gas shut-off valve for about $350 or less. It functions whether or not you are home and offers protection to your own home as well as your entire neighborhood.

• Don't smoke in bed, particularly if you have been drinking.

• Keep an ABC-rated fire extinguisher appropriate for gas and electrical fires in your kitchen.

• If you have a fireplace, be sure there is a spark arrestor on your chimney. Have a chimney sweep clean your chimney annually if you use it regularly.

Near Your Home

• Don't smoke on your deck or use a charcoal barbecue, particularly on windy days.

• If you use gas powered tools like a lawn mower, be sure they have spark arrestors. Avoid using them at all on hot, windy days.

Roadside Ignition

• The most common roadside causes of fires are cigarettes, flares, fireworks, auto fires, hot catalytic convertors, exhaust pipes backed into dry grass, and arson.

• The problem is so serious that The Oakland Wildfire Prevention Assessment District spent the major portion of its vegetation management funds on roadside mowing with priority given to providing access for fire suppression vehicles and egress for residents.

A careless smoker started a fire in this turnout on June 8, 2008, that burned up this draw and singed the townhouses at the top of the hill. Subsequently, the willows in the middle of the draw were reduced by 50 percent and large amounts of dead wood pruned out of them. Ignitable brush was removed to make a firebreak and a fire safe zone above the turnout. The lower branches of surviving trees were removed, and the grass within 20 feet of the roadway was kept short. The 2008 fire, shown on the cover, was ignited by a careless smoker in this turnout.

Fire Prevention Tip #2:
Make Fire Prevention a Year-Round Activity

In the East Bay and much of California it is useful to think of fire prevention in terms of two seasons. The dry season usually begins in mid-May, after the rains have stopped, and lasts until mid-November, when they begin again. This is the time when ignition and fire suppression are key concerns. While the timing and extent of rains vary greatly from year to year—as do temperature and fog—the wet season typically lasts from mid-November to mid-June and is the best time to manage vegetation. Within the two primary seasons there are activities more appropriate to being done earlier or later. (See Appendix A for monthly fire prevention tips.)

Early in the Dry Season
- Attach exterior hoses.
- Avoid power tools on dry windy days.
- Improve the resistance of your home to embers.
- Create and maintain a non-ignition zone adjacent to structures.
- Clear flammable materials from under decks, stairs, and fences.
- Remove seed heads of pampas grass (Jubata), bagging and removing them.
- Inspect and clean chimney and fireplace.
- Prune out and remove dead wood from plants near structures.

Late in the Dry Season

• Keep plants and mulch in the non-ignition zone moist.

• Keep roof and gutters free of flammable debris such as pine needles.

• Prevent igniting fires with cigarettes, charcoal BBQs, and catalytic converters on your vehicle's exhaust.

• Close windows and skylights when away from home and on red flag days.

• Close all windows and garage door if evacuating.

The Wet Season

There are a number of advantages to working during the wet season. There is often better footing on steep moist slopes than on dry ones. Trees are more tolerant of pruning in the dormant season. More workers are available, and the cooler weather is easier for doing heavy work. The following should be your priorities.

• Maintenance of broom species should begin in December and be completed by April. Pull broom seedlings before they bloom, first from shaded moister areas, then from exposed areas after significant rains. Search for tell-tale yellow flowers to locate invading or surviving plants before their seeds ripen.

• Do major tree thinning/pruning and brush removal/pruning early when there is less fire danger, cutting up and mulching the prunings to hasten decomposition.

• Reduce poison oak while relatively dormant.

• Pickaxe pampas grass roots after rains have softened the root ball.

• Pull thistles.

This is the root of a French broom plant pulled out by hand after winter rains had softened the ground. It does not have the type of root structure that will prevent erosion.

Fire Prevention Tip #3:
Reduce Your Home's Vulnerability to Embers

In a wildfire your home is more likely to burn down as a result of smoldering embers than from any other source. While direct contact by flames provides dramatic newsreels, it usually represents a short, passing pulse of flames that is less likely to ignite your home. In contrast, small embers can remain long after the fire front has passed by, then combine to ignite a fire.

A second common cause of ignition in areas where homes are crowded together is radiated heat that can ignite a structure from a distance of 30 feet or more. Vertical and uppermost surfaces are the most exposed to long-lived heat transfer. Even a small flame close to a window can break it, allowing flames to enter directly into the interior.

The following recommendations apply only to the structure itself. Because the Fire Code applies only to new construction or remodels that comprise 25 percent of the footprint of a house, many structures are not cited as noncompliant despite dangerous conditions. Keep in mind that just because your property passed an inspection doesn't mean it is fire safe. Following are guidelines for each element of a dwelling.

Roofs
• Get a AAA rated roof. Avoid tar and gravel for flat roofs.
• Install bird stops for barrel tiles.
• Clean pine needles and leaves from valleys, crooks, and corners, such as dormers, where the roof intersects with siding.

• Screen areas with 1/8" wire mesh where leaves collect. Embers will collect in the same areas.

• Seal gaps between the roof and the fascia on the underside of eaves, as it is prone to rot.

Chimneys and Furnace Vents

• Install spark arresters as required by law.

• If a fireplace is used frequently, have a chimney sweep clean it annually.

• Close the damper when the fireplace is not in use. This will prevent embers from entering.

• Build a robust fire in the fireplace to burn off pitch in the chimney.

Skylights

• Use rated glass.

• Close open skylights when you leave home.

Gutters

• Clean out pine needles and leaves, particularly in the high fire season, and inspect the roof at the same time.

• Use gutter guards or 1/8" mesh to protect hard-to-service areas.

Vents

• Vents at the ridge and eyebrows are for outflow. Those under the eaves are for inflow and thus more dangerous.

• Screen horizontal vents with fiberglass or metal material.

• Screen soffit vents with 1/8" metal mesh to discourage swallows that build flammable nests in them.

Eaves and Soffits

In wildfires embers will be deflected upward along exterior walls to the overhanging eaves. The eaves are protected by soffits that seal the space and resist fire. Older homes with unprotected eaves are at the greatest risk. Even newer homes with unfinished plywood soffits are at risk.

• Eaves should be sealed with soffits made of fire resistant materials.

Siding

• When choosing new or replacement siding keep in mind that rated walls themselves are fairly resistant to fire, stucco more so. Vinyl may melt and fall off as a result of conducted heat as a fire approaches.

• Decayed wood, usually found at the bottom corners of window sills and decks, ignites easily. Chip it out, caulking any gaps.

• Seal the lower edges of siding and remove any combustibles below it.

Windows

Windows are second only to roofs as a source of fire. A broken or open window dooms the house.

• If possible, install double-pane, tempered glass.

• Install bronze metal screens, which absorb a third of conductive heat.

• Consider using metal roll down shutters on first floor windows, particularly when they face dangerous northeasterly Diablo winds.

• If a fire threatens, move flammables, which can be ignited by conductive heat, away from windows.

Window Coverings

• Non-flammable, heavy drapes of natural fibers are best.

• Avoid lace curtains and synthetics.

Decks and Porches

In general, decks are not as much of a problem as what you put under them or on them. Also keep in mind, the closer a deck is to the ground, the more likely it is to catch fire.

• Box decks in with stucco or 1/8" wire mesh.

• Don't attach lattices, which ignite easily and can ladder fire to sleeping areas or eaves.

• Don't store combustibles such as paint cans, fire wood, and brooms under decks.

• Keep a hose attached to spray the deck or soffits from below if a fire threatens.

• Keep decks clear of combustible furniture, baskets, sculptured twigs, and dried flowers.

• Move flammables inside and away from windows if fire is approaching.

• Be aware that BBQ covers are synthetics that can be ignited by embers, melt, then lead to an intense flame that can ignite a deck.

• Use protective, rated stains or paints to protect wood.

• Use top-rated materials for decking. All heart redwood 2" X 6" decking provides excellent fire resistance but is expensive.

• Eliminate gaps where the deck is attached to the structure.

• Clean intersections of horizontal and vertical surfaces, where leaves and embers collect.

Garages

Garages are usually more vulnerable than the rest of a house and, therefore, warrant extra attention.

• Install an automatic gas shut-off valve in the utility closet to protect against a fire triggered by an earthquake.

• Consider replacing your garage door with a cheaper, lighter, fireproof metal door.

• Weather strip any gaps below a rolling door.

• Use 2" X 4" trim for gaps at the top of the door.

- Use rated windows and screen vents.
- Don't use flammable plywood for utility closet doors.
- Know how to disconnect an automatic door, so you can open it if you need to evacuate in a fire that has led to a power failure.
- When evacuating, remember to close the garage door.

Foundations

- Use 1/8" metal mesh to screen vents. This will also block access to mice.

Wire mesh was stapled to the siding of this house to prevent embers from igniting its unsealed lower edge.

Fences and Gates

- Thicker wood is better. Consider using 1 ½" fencing instead of standard pickets.
- A good alternative to a wood fence is wire on a metal or wood frame with well maintained vines.
- Gates made of non-flammable materials can break the continuity of a flammable fence.
- Stucco pillars also break the continuity of a flammable fence.

• In addition to eliminating a fire danger, removing a fence may provide better security by eliminating cover for burglars.

• Direct sprinkling on a fence can create decayed, easily ignitable wood.

• Leaving a gap at the bottom of a fence helps prevent decay.

• Metal, masonry or stucco elements can create a barrier where a wood fence attaches to a house.

• Never store combustibles against a fence.

Fire Prevention Tip #4:
Maintain a Non-Ignition Zone Adjacent to Your Home

It is extremely important to create and maintain a non-ignition zone in the five feet immediately adjacent to your home so embers will not start a fire here.

Remove Combustibles from Vulnerable Areas

As previously noted, overhangs, eaves, decks, stairs and ground level vents are particularly vulnerable, so these are the first place to look.

• Remove anything near windows or glass doors, including window boxes.

• Remove firewood, construction debris, brooms, flammable decorations, and wood trellises from adjacent areas.

Use Non-Flammable Materials

Whenever possible, replace burnable materials around your home with non-flammable alternatives.

• Pavement, paving stones, walkways, driveways, rocks, pebbles, concrete, tile, stucco, water features, and soft cement-like materials such as composite granite, all contribute to making your home defensible.

• Bare ground, which also favors native bees, can also help.

• Fences of wire, cyclone fencing, iron gates, wire gates, and green fences are all preferable to wood.

• Walls of piled rock, thick wood retaining walls, and earthen berms all provide barriers to the spread of fire.

• Recycled plastics, small lumber and uncapped lattices increase the risk of fire.

Manage Vegetation

In a wildfire, most plants burn within 90 seconds. To reduce fire danger you need to be conscious about where you put plants, how you space them, and, most importantly, how you maintain them. You need to be able to rake underneath them easily. By limiting fuels close to your structure, you minimize heat output and ignition.

• Break up continuity by providing both vertical and horizontal spacing between plants and between plants and chimney outlets, windows, eaves, overhangs, decks, stairs, fencing, and vents.

• Trees don't usually burn by themselves. Eliminate brush beneath trees and ground fuels that ladder into them. Remove lower branches, dead or drying branches, and peeling bark. Prune branches away from chimneys, windows, overhangs, and vents. Decrease the density of crowns.

• Keep roofs, especially corners, free of pine needles, particularly in high fire season and on red flag days. Even redwood debris can burn in a drought.

• Open up brush by pruning or removing hedges from under eaves, decks, and windows. Flames can be three times the height of a plant.

Mulch

Ground covers can provide living mulch in the non-ignition zone. By keeping soil bare, you also help native bees nest, since they can't penetrate deep mulch. Farther from a structure, mulching can help weed control and put organic material or moisture back into the soil. Keep in mind that larger chips may roll down steep hills.

Don't mulch within five feet of a structure. It is important to be able rake debris from under plants and the lower, unsealed edges of siding.

• Avoid pine needles and shredded cedar—even shredded

An excellent example of an attractive non-ignition zone consisting of pebbles, rocks, pavement stones, thick wood, and-well spaced fire resistant plants.

redwood or pine bark pellets—since cigarette butts or embers can ignite these.

• A good mulch alternative is pea gravel, which keeps plants cooler and thriving.

Good Fire Resistant Plant Choices

• Herb gardens
• Almost anything in a pot
• High mineral content plants (gray), such as geraniums, cyclamen and bulbs
• Plants with little dead matter, such as succulents
• Plants with thick, large leaves, such as camellias and rhododendrons
• Plants with a high moisture content
• Ferns and other plants with an open, airy form and low fuel load
• Flowering annuals with a brief growing period and little dead wood

• Some favorable choices include Western redbud, Marguerite daisy, Pineapple guava, and Oleander (which is very difficult to ignite even if you try to).

Characteristics of Less Fire Resistant Plants
• Plants with aromatic oils
• Plants that create a buildup of dead matter
• Plants with tiny leaves that lose moisture and ignite easily
• Particularly bad choices include Juniper (called a green gas can by firefighters), Rosemary (develops lots of highly flammable dead wood), Blue gum eucalyptus (highly flammable debris, leaves, and bark), French, Scotch and Spanish broom, Monterey pine (easily ignited by radiated heat with a lot of dead wood and dropped needles), California lilac *(Ceanothus)*, Pride of Madeira (very woody, spreads voraciously to surrounding areas).

This photograph demonstrates the importance of a non-ignition zone. Highly flammable prostrate coyote bush *(baccharis)* and live oak seedlings were foolishly planted close to balconies in this area during landscaping after the 1991 firestorm. When a fire ignited these fuels in 2008, firefighters had to eliminate them with their backs literally against the wall.

Fire Prevention Tip #5:
Create Defensible Space around Your Home

Actions taken by homeowners before a wildfire occurs can make the difference between a home surviving or not. This section focuses on what you can do to:

1. Give yourself time to evacuate.

2. Provide firefighters the opportunity to effectively defend your house.

3. Encourage firefighters to consider your house salvageable when they perform structure triage.

4. Increase the odds your home may survive on its own when firefighting resources are overwhelmed.

What Is Defensible Space?

Defensible space is the area between a house and an oncoming wildfire where the vegetation has been modified to reduce the wildfire threat. The aim is to reduce the intensity of the wildfire as it nears a home.

The vegetation surrounding a home can have considerable influence upon its survivability and that of its neighbors. All vegetation, including plants native to the area and ornamental plants, is potential fire fuel. If this vegetation is properly modified and maintained, a wildfire can be slowed, the height of flames shortened, and the amount of heat reduced, all of which reduce the chance of a home being consumed by fire.

The California Fire Code requires homeowners to maintain a defensible space of at least 30 feet around their homes and sometimes up to 100 feet or even further, depending on property lines. This code was developed at a national level to protect against a moving fire front at the wildland-urban interface. It primarily targets areas where homes are on relatively flat lots that are adequately separated from neighboring houses. Such lots are rare in the Oakland hills that form the focus of this guidebook.

Conditions in the Oakland Hills

Oakland Hills residents live in a densely populated wildland-urban intermix, an area where there are steep hills, little flat land, and narrow winding streets that frequently terminate in dead-ends. Many homes are built 10 to 20 feet apart on narrow lots that may extend for a few hundred feet up or down slope. In the Oakland Hills dangerous northeasterly Diablo winds tend to blow flames downhill, whereas fires in most areas spread more rapidly uphill.

The weather in the Oakland Hills is also unusual. Vegetation management work can be done with less hazard of ignition during the wet winter season because there is rarely any snow or freezing. These conditions also hasten decomposition of cut materials, a valuable advantage since controlled burns are seldom advisable in the area. During the summer, frequent thick fog generates dripping from the tree canopy that moistens the underlying soil.

In 2004 voters created the Oakland Wildfire Prevention Assessment District, funded by Oakland hills residents for the Oakland hills, that steadily decreased fire dangers and became a respected model for wildland–urban interface fire districts throughout the nation.

Scope of this Section

Tip #4 focuses on the first five feet surrounding a house, the non-ignition zone. This section focuses entirely on what homeowners can do to manage vegetation on their own land in the lean, green and clean zone beyond the non-ignition zone. This may extend 30 feet from their home or even a few hundred feet into what might appropriately be called a buffer or wildland fuel reduction zone.

The strategies appropriate for your property will vary greatly and depend on the specific characteristics of that property. Nevertheless, the tips that follow are meant to be those that homeowners can implement themselves. Homeowners have access to more methods with fewer restrictions than those working on public lands. They are intimately familiar with their property and can closely monitor it, maintaining it as needed when needed.

Seven Steps to Creating an Effective Defensible Space

1. Evaluate Your Effective Defensible Space

The distance your property extends to your property line from the foundation of your house will probably vary in different directions. Consider the different kinds of vegetation present, including invasive exotics, and the differences in slope. Determine, as well, the direction a wildfire is most likely to come from. Take into account the danger of wooden fences and other separate structures, such as gazebos, and also the positive contribution of driveways, patios, and swimming pools.

2. Provide for Driveway Clearance

Reduce vegetation at least 10 feet from both sides of the driveway to provide an adequate evacuation route as well as access for firefighters. If possible, overhanging branches and power lines should be removed or raised to provide at least 15 feet of vertical clearance.

3. Create a Lean, Clean, and Green Area Extending 5 to 30 Feet from the House

For most homeowners, this area is also the residential landscape. It often has irrigation, is planted with ornamental vegetation, and is regularly maintained. Your first goal here is to eliminate easily ignitable fuels ("kindling") near the house. This will help prevent embers from starting a fire in your yard. The second goal is to keep fire intensity low if anything does ignite. With proper management of vegetation a fire won't be able to generate enough heat to set your home on fire.

4. Remove Dead Vegetation

Dead vegetation is particularly dangerous and includes dead and dying standing trees, recently fallen trees, dead native and ornamental shrubs, dead branches, and dried grass, weeds and flowers. Fallen trees that are embedded into the ground and located more than 30 feet from the house can be left in place, but exposed branches should be removed.

Pay particular attention to flammable ground fuels under bushes or trees. Pine needles and leaves should be removed from the non-ignition zone in late spring unless they accumulate on the ground beyond the non-ignition zone as long as they do not create a fire hazard. Don't allow fallen needles and leaves to exceed a depth of three inches within 30 feet of your house.

5. Remove Ladder Fuels

Vegetation that can carry a fire from low-growing plants into taller plants is called ladder fuel. Remove lower branches up to 6 to 10 feet above the ground, but not more than a third of the height of the tree. Shrubs growing near or under the drip-line should also be removed. Irrigated, well-maintained lawn and flower beds, as well as low-growing native ground covers, can be kept under a tree's drip-line as long as they won't allow a fire to ignite the tree.

6. Create a Separation between Trees and Shrubs

A small grassland opening onto a field of coyote brush

An example of defensible space at the top of a steep slope where erosion is a concern. Note the separation between groups of tree crowns that soften the rain and provide fog drip. Ladder fuels were removed but their roots left intact. A mixture of naturally occurring native plants serving as ground cover has been preserved.

can provide a beautiful, accessible, botanically rich and fuel-reduced pocket within a mosaic of brush and trees.

In contrast, Monterey pine, California lilac, and coyote bush in dense stands pose a significant wildfire threat. These need to be thinned to create space between them. On a flat or gently sloping terrain more than 30 feet from a house, individual shrubs or small clumps of shrubs should be separated from one another by at least twice the height of the average shrub. On steeper slopes, the separation distance should be greater. Remove shrubs or prune them to reduce their height and diameter. They may be pruned in rotating years to preserve their roots for erosion control.

On flat to gently sloping terrain more than 30 feet from a house, provide an average separation between the canopies of trees of at least 10 feet. Greater distances between trees or groupings of trees is recommended on steep slopes. Also, keep in mind that conditions differ greatly depending on whether a slope is northeast facing (with less sun exposure, moister soil, and lush desirable groundcover) or southwest facing (with more sun exposure, dryer soil, and more ignitable plants such as broom and coyote bush).

7. Maintain Your Defensible Space

Maintaining the defensible space is an ongoing year round activity that will vary significantly from year to year depending on the weather. Plants grow, and flammable vegetation needs to be routinely removed and disposed of properly. Before each fire season, reevaluate your property using the previous six steps and implement the necessary defensible space recommendations.

A professional crew cleared dense brush and pruned trees up to 300 feet below this townhouse in the direct path of dangerous northeast Diablo winds.

Fire Prevention Tip #6:
Create a Wildland Fuel Reduction Buffer Zone

Four years after the catastrophic 1991 Firestorm in the Oakland and Berkeley Hills, the Vegetation Management Consortium definitively stated, "Manage the vegetation in the hills or, as history and fire science has shown us, it will again burn catastrophically."

They did not suggest clearing all vegetation within 10 feet of a road or 30 feet of any building or ignoring biological values. Rather, they recommended a complex and nuanced approach to vegetation management for different types of plant communities. The aim of these recommendations was to reduce and separate fuels so that they would be more manageable when wildfires occur.

This approach, if carried out in a thoughtful and enlightened way, can yield wonderful results. Instead of being an environmental negative, with cleared bare earth, fire safety guidelines can encourage healthy, beautiful, and botanically diverse wildlands.

Grasslands

While the overall fire hazard for grasslands is moderate, the actual danger in any one location depends greatly on the height and density of grasses, weeds, and forbs (herbs with a soft, rather than permanent woody stem), and their relationship to brush. In tall grass (above knee level) flame heights may reach 12 feet or more. Tall-grass fires are hazardous to firefighters, burning up to 10 times as high, fast, and hot as short-grass fires.

To reduce the fire hazard in grasslands:

- Shorten grasses.
- Manage potential ignition sites.
- Encourage native perennial grasses.
- Encourage less flammable groundcovers.
- Break up the continuity of the grasses with firebreaks, low stone walls, earthen berms, or horizontal lines of shrubs.

Mowing at a height that preserves low-lying ground covers such as wild strawberries, California wild blackberry, wild cucumber and ferns is recommended. Hand pulling and mowing are preferable to using goats, which eat everything, including desirable plants. A line or island of shrubs may slow the spread of grass fires because they have a higher combustion temperature. Native bunch grasses are less fire prone, less contiguous, need less water, stay green longer, and have deep roots that help prevent erosion.

Brush and Scrub Dominant Communities

Brush and scrub became dominant in the Oakland hills when grasslands were no longer managed with grazing and periodic burning as housing replaced them. The fire hazard brush and scrub presents is usually described as *highest* or *most extreme*. This is particularly true of climax stands of tall coyote bush and broom species, which may reach 10 to 12 feet and produce tremendous heat and flames 69 feet high.

To reduce the fire hazard in brush:
- Shorten overall height of shrubs.
- Remove invasive exotic species.
- Remove or reduce dead materials and litter.
- Separate islands of taller shrubs.
- Encourage natural succession to grasslands or woodlands.

After development pressure, the biggest threats to California's beleaguered but still fabulously rich wildlands are invasive exotic species like French, Scotch and Spanish broom, pampas grass, blue gum eucalyptus, Monterey pine, and blackwood acacia. All these seriously increase fuel loads while also usurping native habitats. Removing and discouraging these pyrophytic weeds can make room for less fire-prone local native plant communities.

Forests and Riparian Communities

In these areas ground fuels may need to be reduced and separated, especially tall exotic grasses and brush, so fires don't consolidate into massive fronts. Ladder fuels under trees are important to manage, as they are the most likely source of ignition to trees. Dense fire chimneys and tree crowns need to be judiciously interrupted or thinned.

Native oaks, though less likely to form fire brands, often contain many dead branches that can ignite and burn intensely. If choked with heavy brush, ladder fuels, and dead branches, a great old oak may be ignited and propagate a fire. Once the brush has been thinned and shortened, such a tree may provide a natural, shaded firebreak, representing a value preserved.

Pine trees, especially Monterey pines, produce a lot of dead needles and litter and contain turpentine, making them easily ignitable by radiant heat in the absence of direct flame. Once ignited, winds carry storms of firebrands to roofs and downwind areas.

Blue gum eucalyptus requires considerable maintenance because of its flammable bark and detritus. Even native California lilac or elderberries may be a hazard because of considerable buildup of dead wood in their branches. Willows may produce a great amount of dead branches than can ladder a fire up a dry drainage area.

To optimize results, each tree or group of trees should be considered individually, whether native or not. Most trees provide needed shade, discourage the growth of flammable brush underneath, soften the effect of heavy rains on erosion, and catch fog to produce life-giving fog drip, sequester carbon, and turn carbon monoxide into oxygen. Nevertheless, trees are often planted without anticipating what their growth will be and what maintenance will be required.

Be the Steward of Your Own Property

It is crucial to understand that fire prevention requires an ongoing effort that involves patience, commitment, and regular monitoring of your property. You need to be the steward of your own land, caring for it on a long-term basis, informed by frequent field observations and knowledge, as well as the research and work of others.

A wide buffer zone was created on this steep slope at the top of a fire chimney below thriving trees. Thick brush and dead willow limbs were removed gradually over several years to reduce the number of decomposition piles left on the hill at one time and to minimize erosion.

Appendix A
Monthly Fire Prevention Tips

January	Begin Eradication of Broom Species
February	Plan for Fire Safe Spring Planting
March	Prepare for Annual Inspection
April	Begin Seasonal Mowing of Flash Fuels
May	Remove Close-In Combustibles
June	Prevent Ignition
July	Have an Evacuation Plan
August	Evacuate Your Home If All Else Fails
September	Maintain and Review May-August Tips
October	Plan for the Wet Season
November	Consider Christmas Gift Ideas
December	Consider Decomposition Piles

January   Begin Eradication of Broom Species

It is more effective to eradicate French, Scotch, and Spanish broom during the rainy season since plants with stems up to one inch in diameter can easily be pulled out by the roots without risk of spreading seeds. Large plants can be hauled to the curb for removal or cut up into piles that will decompose rapidly on site.

For plants with larger stems, cut part way through with a pruning saw, then break the stem downward and strip the bark. The remainder of the bark can then be pealed down to the ground, leaving a bare stump to treat directly with a few squirts of liquid Roundup.

Work upward on a slope, leaving a stump of at least four inches to provide a foothold and make it easy to re-cut with a single stroke if there is any subsequent re-sprouting. Plants with smaller stems can be cut with loppers, twisting the loppers when you complete the cut, then peeling the bark downward. Alternatively you can simply break the stem and strip it downward by hand. On mild slopes and flatter ground you can use a weed wrench or pickaxe to dig a plant out by the roots.

Once the first cut of broom is made in an area, your goal will be to prevent plants from dropping seeds, thus depleting the existing seed stock over time. It's important to patrol the treated area regularly during the rainy season, pulling out new seedlings and treating any surviving plants. Look carefully for plants hidden within shrubs such as coyote bush or poison oak. If seedlings are dense, you can rake them with a pruning saw, or you can wait until the survivors are a few feet tall.

Inspect your entire property in April and May, looking for the telltale yellow blossoms of flowering broom that indicate missed plants or the invasion of a new area. Broom tends to spread downhill to contiguous areas, so look uphill for surviving plants above the area you have cleared that may be reseeding the area.

After a well-performed first cut, when the bulk of the biomass is removed, and after meticulous upkeep the next year, maintenance will become much easier. Periods of rain may lead to a flourish of new seedlings, so it pays to be obsessive compulsive in removing any new blooming broom.

Compared to public lands where contractors must be scheduled well in advance to do this work without knowing exactly what may be required when, private property owners have the advantage of being able to check their property frequently for surviving plants and remove them at their convenience.

February   Plan for Fire Safe Spring Planting

Since property conditions vary greatly, a simple list of what is good or bad to plant in the defensible space near a home is inadequate. Nonetheless, here are a few general guidelines to consider.

Trees

Remember, trees grow. Plant smaller trees that won't overwhelm your structure. Consider a flowering plum, western redbud, pineapple guava, or trees such as Japanese maples that tolerate pruning. Avoid pines (particularly Monterey pines), blue gum eucalyptus, and palm trees. California lilac *(Ceanothus),* although native, has a short life span and can become a fire hazard as it fills up with dead wood.

Space trees out to separate the crowns. Trees don't normally burn by themselves; so eliminate ground fuels and brush that might carry fire into the tree. To simplify maintenance don't plant tall trees near your structure, in front of a window, or along the border of your property.

Shrubs

Avoid juniper (called green gas by firefighters), all species of broom, and pampas grass *(Cortaderia jubata)*. Rosemary develops lots of dead wood and becomes highly flammable, but well maintained individual plants may be used. Pride of Madeira manifests similar characteristics and can also broadcast seeds out of your garden into nearby wild areas. Choose plants with high mineral content (indicated by a gray color), little dead matter, thick leaves, high moisture content, and an open, airy form. Well cared for camellias, azaleas and rhododendrons are good choices. Plants with aromatic oils are usually a bad choice, though individual oleanders are surprisingly difficult to ignite. Manzanita, though native, can burn with high intensity.

Garden Plants

Consider an herb garden and almost anything in a pot. Avoid ivy where it may spread into nearby wildlands or become difficult to control. Geraniums, cyclamen and other bulbs, cactus, succulents, and flowering annuals are good choices. *Myoporums,* a genus of flowering plants in the figwort family, are small shrubs or small trees that can take full sun and tolerate hot, dry weather. *Myoporum Prostratum* is a dense low cover plant with creeping roots. Though locally invasive, it is desirable in areas with fast growing grasses because it can survive mowing above it.

Vertical Gardens

A good way to create privacy screening is to create a wire mesh fence with well-maintained vines or other plants growing up it. You should be aware, however, that a screen used for privacy also gives potential burglars a place to hide.

Mulch Alternatives

For fire prevention, what is under plants is extremely important, and mulches can themselves become a source of ignition. Consider using rocks, pebbles, or paving stones instead.

March   Prepare for Annual Inspection

Annual inspections of private properties in the Oakland Hills may be scheduled early in the year to allow time for abatement before the highest hazard fire season arrives, with priority given to habitually non-compliant properties.

Inspections are performed by Oakland Fire Department engine companies under the supervision of fire inspectors, who monitor the firemen's performance and follow-up on properties found out of compliance. Inspectors, who are paid out of City funds, may meet with homeowners to develop reasonable plans for compliance.

Most confusion about the inspections results from the fact that the existing Fire Code was developed as a national code that was later adopted by the state of California . The state in turn required Oakland to adopt the code as written. Nevertheless, what might be appropriate for Idaho or Arizona is often not appropriate for Oakland , and case by case exceptions are allowed.

For example, it is often not practical to trim every tree branch the specified minimum of 10 feet from any roof, chimney, and structure, or to remove all dead or dying branches from trees, or to remove all tree limbs within six feet of the ground. Inspectors are realistic and may ask to see limbs cut back a few feet from any structure, particularly near openings such as windows, vents and eaves, from under decks and stairs, and back from chimneys, stovepipe outlets, and gutters. They usually find that limbing a smaller tree one-fourth its height is sufficient.

Inspectors are concerned about what is under the tree and how it is maintained, as ground fuels can ignite easily and spread fire into the tree or an overhanging deck. Dense growths of juniper and overgrown rosemary are likely to be cited. Plants should be spaced apart, have an airy form, and be free of dead wood. Mulch itself can become a fire hazard when it dries out and should be raked back at least a foot from the side of the house and from combustible fencing.

Inspectors are also concerned about the accumulation of leaves, needles or other dead or drying vegetation on the roof. Keep in mind that immediately after clearing your roof, the detritus begins to build up again. Consider installing commercially available gutter guards and be sure to remove accumulations during the highest hazard months of September and October, though trimming, tree removal, or tree replacement might be preferable.

Finally, don't assume that the fact you passed an inspection means your home is fire safe. The fire code and inspections are limited in scope. They don't address the structure itself, which is why the blue "Recommends" section was added to the annual notice.

This area along Hiller Drive had become an inpenetrable tangle of French broom by 1998. Maintenance now consists of pulling a few broom seedlings during the wet season, pruning coyote bushes back every year on a rotating basis, and mowing the annual grasses in April. Native bunch grasses are thriving.

April   Begin Seasonal Mowing of Flash Fuels

Flash fuels consist of grasses and dried weeds that ignite easily and can spread fire quickly to engulf a home in flames. Firefighters have died fighting grass fires when the wind changed, and they became surrounded by flames.

April is a good time to make sure your property is in compliance with the fire code by mowing these fuels to six inches or less within 30 feet of your structure.

Be careful not to start a fire while trying to prevent it. A two cycle engine on a mower or steel blades on a weed whacker striking a rock can cause sparks. Do not mow on hot, windy days when the grass is fully dried, and always have a hose or fire suppression tool nearby.

Depending on the rains, mowing may be started as early as April. Usually, it should be completed by early June. You can selectively hand pull small quantities of flash fuels out by the roots.

In years with robust rains, grasses can bolt to unusual heights. So, it may help to weed whack the grass early in spring when it is two to three feet high. When grass grows taller it is more difficult to cut. Cutting early allows you to mulch it and leave it on site, and thus avoid the difficulty and expense of removing it from steep slopes. Early cutting also prevents seeding and favors low-lying ground cover and desirable bunch grasses.

Consider following up with a later mowing close to the ground in strategic close-in areas and then raking and removing the cut grass to create a fire break.

May   **Remove Close-In Combustibles**

As the high fire hazard season approaches, this is a good time to remove combustible materials near your home. None of the following recommended actions involve using tools that may start a fire.

• Attach exterior hoses.

• Remove combustibles on and under decks, overhangs, stairs and fences.

• Keep leaves and other flammable debris away from lawn and deck furniture, barbecues, dog houses, children's play structures, or toys.

• Remove dead wood and ground litter from close-in plants.

• Rake mulch, pine needles and leaves at least two feet away from your home's foundation and from wooden fences.

• Cut vegetation and branches back at least three feet from windows and glass doors.

• Screen foundation vents with 1/8" wire mesh.

• Keep gutters and roofs free of pine needles and leaves, particularly in the corners. It is important to check these areas after high winds that may lead to a considerable accumulation of dry pine needles from nearby trees.

• Attach street address numbers to your home that are clearly visible from the road. These should be in a contrasting color and at least four inches high.

June   Prevent Fires from Starting

Almost all wildfires in the East Bay hills are caused by people. Report any suspicious behavior immediately to the police or fire department.

Earthquake Hazards

It is extremely important, for both you and your neighbors, that you have an automatic shut off valve installed on your gas line. This works 24/7, even when you are out of town. Plumbers will install one for about $300 to $350. Be careful not to bump the valve when putting things in your utility closet. It helps to know how to safely relight the pilot light on your water heater when you accidently bump it.

Within the Home

Smoking in bed, particularly when combined with drinking, is the most common cause of fire in the home. Kitchen grease fires are also common, so be sure you have a fire extinguisher close at hand in the kitchen. The law requires you to have a spark arrestor on your chimney. Depending on how often you use your fireplace, you should also have your chimney swept every year or so.

Near the Home

The covers on large barbecues are usually made of a synthetic material that can be ignited by firebrands, melt onto the deck, and ignite it. The grease pan can ignite if not cleaned out regularly. Charcoal barbecues are dangerous because of the sparks they put out, particularly on windy days, and they are illegal on decks. Never smoke outside your home or use gas-powered lawnmowers, weed whackers or chain saws on windy days.

Nearby Spot Fires

You may be able to put out spot fires started by flying

embers outside the perimeter of the main fire with a hose, fire extinguisher, entry mat or car mat. Fire rakes, fire suppression flap tools, and backpack water sprayers are available from mail order suppliers such as gemplers.com or benmeadows.com.

Roadsides and Trailsides

Cigarettes led to the 2008 Tunnel Road fire and a fire above the North Oakland Athletic Field before that. Catalytic convertors can ignite dry grass when cars are backed into it. Flares put out for an accident ignited a fire on Grizzly Peak Road not long ago. Inadequately extinguished cooking fires led to the 1991 firestorm, the Angora fire at Lake Tahoe, the Inverness fire at Point Reyes, and the Rim fire near Yosemite.

July   Make an Evacuation Plan

The first step in any evacuation plan is to designate a meeting place for your family outside of your neighborhood in case they are not together when a disaster strikes.

Emergency Contacts

The next step is to enter important contacts in each family member's cell phone. Also, identify someone who lives outside of the potential hazard area for friends and family to contact for updates on your situation. Ideally, this should be someone in a different part of California or even in another state. This is particularly important in a major earthquake. To keep phone lines from becoming overloaded, ask that person to phone or text relatives and friends located out of the area.

Records

Keep originals or duplicates of important documents such as passports, wills, birth certificates, marriage certificates and insurance policies in an off-site location, not a safe. Digitalized photographs and scanned documents can be stored online. Take photographs (movies preferred) of the inside of your home and valuables to substantiate possible insurance claims. Include copies of receipts for unusually expensive items such as jewelry, paintings, antiques, computers and cameras.

Identify Items to Take

Place family photos and other irreplaceable items in clearly identified boxes so that you can quickly load them into your car before evacuating. Have a small duffel bag or backpack packed with emergency non-flammable clothing for you and your family. Keep your daily medications, personal hygiene items, and a flashlight together with a bag nearby for carrying them.

Pre-Plan for Pets

Prepare a kit with food, leashes, and collars. Include current photos. Consider a microchip for identification.

Gas, Electricity, and Water

Learn how to shut off your gas, electricity and water, and how to open your garage door manually. Have fire extinguishers in your house and car.

Radio

Have a battery-powered radio to keep track of the progress of a fire and a cell phone charger in your car.

Evacuation Routes

Identify all possible evacuation routes in advance. A bicycle may be an alternative to a car. The Fire Department cannot recommend routes in advance because some routes may not be safe and others may be blocked off for firefighter access. You should also plan for alternative exits from your home in case the most obvious choice is blocked by fire or debris. Consider purchasing an emergency fire escape ladder you can hang from a deck railing.

August   Prepare for a Safe Evacuation

Keep your car keys, wallet, glasses and cell phone in a dedicated location en route to your garage so you don't waste time looking for them in an emergency.

Clothing

Wear cotton or wool clothing, a long sleeve shirt, and long pants. Synthetic materials can melt onto skin. Wear leather gloves and boots, a cloth hat or safety helmet, and goggles. Have a face mask in your glove compartment that you can wear to minimize smoke inhalation, especially in areas of burning poison oak.

Urgent Evacuation

Be ready for a quick getaway. Know how to open your garage door manually. Park your car facing outward toward the street with the keys in the ignition. Evacuate children, the disabled, the elderly, and pets to the location you have previously identified. Do not stay behind if you know a fire is heading your way.

Close All Openings to Your Home's Interior

Reduce the chance of flames entering your home by closing all windows, patio doors, skylight vents, and garage doors. Move combustibles such as synthetic drapes, furniture and decorative items away from windows. Close interior doors. Leave all doors and windows unlocked and leave the lights on for firefighter access.

Move Nearby Combustibles Away

Most common nearby combustibles include lawn furniture, cloth or plastic awnings, barbecues, and portable propane tanks. Those on a deck can be moved inside the house.

Extinguish Spot Fires If Time Permits

If you have time, fill a waterproof garbage can with water and place a bucket near it so someone can dip into it to put out spot fires from embers. Exterior hoses should have been hooked up at the beginning of the dry season. The mat in your car can be used for smothering small fires. Smoldering fires caused by embers frequently flare up long after the fire front has passed by. When fire personnel must focus on the fire front, you can help greatly by extinguishing embers in advance of the flames.

Upon Evacuation

Close your garage door when you evacuate. Many homes were lost in the Angora fire at Lake Tahoe because homeowners panicked and left without closing their garage doors, allowing embers to blow into their open garage and ignite their homes.

September   Maintain Fire Safety and Review Previous Tips

If you have already implemented the recommended fire prevention tips, you should be in pretty good shape as the high fire season occurs. This is the time to maintain the fire safe measures you have put in place and to review key parts of your plan.

Maintain Clearance of Close-In Combustibles

Keep your gutters and roofs free of accumulated pine needles and leaves, especially after strong winds have deposited them on your roof. Rake them back from under your decks, under your stairs, and under your close-in plants. Check to make sure you haven't left brooms, flammable decorations, or flammable debris where they could be ignited by fire brands.

Prevent Fires

Don't smoke in bed or outside your home. Don't use a charcoal barbecue. Be sure the drip pan on your gas barbecue has been cleaned out. Remove the flammable cover of your barbecue and store it inside. Don't park your car where the catalytic convertor could ignite flash fuels. Be sure your outside hoses are connected and any fire suppression tools are readily available.

Be Prepared for Possible Evacuation

Be sure to leave your car keys, wallet, glasses and cell phone in a dedicated location en route to your garage, where you should have a plastic bag containing a face mask, chalk to leave a message on your door, and non-flammable clothing. Practice opening and closing your garage door manually. Place a few weeks supply of essential medications in a bag where you can readily access them. Review the short list of valuables you would want to take with you, post the list, and have appropriate containers available. Have a kit of pet food, leashes, collars and pictures readily available in your garage.

Critical Reminders

You and your neighbors should know how to turn off each other's gas and water, as you may not be home when a fire occurs. Close your windows and skylight vents when away from home, particularly so on the hot, dry days you're most likely to leave them open. When evacuating, don't forget to close your garage door and all windows, but do leave doors unlocked and the lights on for firefighter access.

October   Plan for the Wet Season

Fire prevention is a year-round job, particularly in the Mediterranean climate common in California. There is considerable overlap in these activities depending on weather, type of vegetation, and slope. Most recommended vegetation management is best done during the wet season, which typically lasts from mid-November through May. These months are favorable because:

• Rains nourish seeds and seedlings.
• Steep, moist slopes provide better footing than dry ones.
• There is little risk of power tools igniting a fire.
• Trees and brush tolerate pruning better when dormant.
• Leaf drop reduces the amount of debris to be removed.
• Cooler weather makes it easier for workers to do this strenuous work.
• More workers are available in this "off season."
• Rains facilitate decomposition of cuttings.
• There is less chance of spreading ripened seeds.

In December and January:
• Seed, sow and plant desirables.
• Thin, mow, or remove relatively dormant poison oak and hemlock.
• Prune and thin trees and brush, using decomposition piles where appropriate.

Tasks for February and March include:
• Pull seedlings of broom and other weeds.
• Spray thistle with bleach or Roundup while its leaves are spread flat on the ground; dig up root balls of pampas grass.
• Improve trail access.

Tasks for April and May include:
• Eradicate any remaining flowering broom.
• Pull thistles and unwanted grasses.

November   Christmas Gift Ideas

These are gifts every family could use:

- Kitchen fire extinguisher for grease fires.
- Outside fire extinguisher for BBQ fires.
- Escape ladder for bedroom when escape route is blocked.

Here are some gift ideas for a person active in fire prevention:

- Fire suppression tools to put out spot fires: 15 gallon backpack for water; fire flap on a pole; fire rake; and Pulaski fire tool. These are all available from benmeadows.com or gemplers.com.

- Under-the-bed earthquake survival kit. You can make this yourself. Include a crowbar, light stick that requires no batteries, face mask, escape ladder, whistle, cloth hat and jacket or sweatshirt, old hiking shoes, leather gloves, protective goggles.

- Stihl gas powered chain saw. This costs about $200 and is by far the best. Protective chaps and proper headgear are a must.

- Good loppers, hand pruning saws and a variety of weed whackers and extended pruning saws for tree limbs.

- A small 29-pound generator to power up your cell phone, computer, and lights for $700.

- Chain saw boots with cleats for steep slopes can be obtained from gemplers.com. They are waterproof and high enough to keep annoying pointed grass seeds from getting in.

December   Consider Decomposition Piles

It is not economically reasonable to remove cut brush and trees from large, steep properties. When thinning or reducing a stand of Monterey pines, for example, it may cost more to remove the cuttings than to log the trees. As an alternative, gathering the resulting debris in a degradation pile can reduce the fire hazard by as much as 90 percent. This is also true for broom, poison oak, coyote brush, and live oak prunings.

A proper degradation pile is a dense mass of cut-up limbs no more than 18 inches high and six feet in diameter. It should be separated by at least 10 feet from other such piles, with no surrounding highly flammable fuel and far enough away so that it won't ignite a tree or structure. If possible locate it where it can help prevent erosion. Even if an ember ignites such a pile, the fire will be unlikely to spread.

This technique saves money that can better be used to extend the fire-safe zone. It works best on a northeast facing slope where there is likely to be more natural groundcover such as California blackberry, wild strawberry, ferns, wild cucumber or native bunch grasses. Willow trunks and eucalyptus are slow to decompose compared to pines and brush.

Such decomposition piles provide habitat for small animals and insects that may in turn provide a food source for birds. They are particularly appropriate to the East Bay hills, where mild, wet winters facilitate decomposition. In the Sierras, on the other hand, such fuels freeze in the winter and have to be burned off in spring.

Appendix B—Problem Invasive Plants

Monterey Pine

Monterey pine *(Pinus radiata; Pinaceae)* is a beautiful tree that can grow to 60 feet in only 15 years, making it a popular landscape plant in California. However, it's the highest fire hazard tree around. It is literally a turpentine factory that ignites easily by conduction of heat even without a bare flame being present. Burning needles and branches are easily carried airborne, spreading fire downwind for long distances. As they rushed to evacuate in the face of a horizontal blowtorch of embers, survivors of the Oakland Hills Firestorm of 1991 could hear these trees exploding in fire.

Drought and frequent infestation by bark beetles and pine pitch canker increase the susceptibility of these trees to fire as they age. Moreover, they are relatively short-lived, with an average lifespan of 40 to 60 years. Aging trees often drop large branches, split apart, or fall on roads, buildings or parked cars.

In addition, as these trees mature, they produce a rapid build-up of dead branches and pine needles under the trees that ignites easily and spreads the fire to the dead lower branches, creating a fuel ladder. The mature trees burn with intense heat to heights beyond the reach of firefighters' equipment.

Although native to the Central Coast from San Mateo to San Luis Obispo counties, the Monterey pine is not native to the East Bay, and is of little value to wildlife. It crowds out native plants by depriving them of sunlight and covers the ground with a thick layer of decomposing duff. When it burns it produces a dense crop of seedlings. Other pine trees, even redwoods, exhibit some similar characteristics.

There are two basic strategies for dealing with Monterey pine.

1. Eradication

Eradication is the most cost-effective solution. Once cut, these trees do not regrow from stumps so no herbicide is needed. The wood is relatively soft and easy to cut with loppers, a pruning saw, or a chain saw. It is urgent they be cut when small, as they can grow four feet a year with a proportionate increase in the cost of removal. Remove trees from underneath balconies, decks, and roof overhangs. Remove specimens from ridge tops or near the urban interface to prevent embers from igniting distant spot fires.

Medium branches can be thrown stepwise down a hill to a dumpster and cut up with a chain saw for compacting. Larger trunks can be winched down a hill. Trunks will decompose over years and may be left in separate piles where appropriate. Trunks as much as two feet in diameter were found rotting and turning into soil 10 years after the Oakland Firestorm.

2. Maintenance

Management requires annual maintenance and pruning. If you choose to leave a tree in place, it is important to create vertical separation between the tree canopy and surface fuels below. Remove lower branches for a third of the height of the tree or up to 6 feet. Remove dead branches and reduce the duff layer. Create separation between groupings of trees, thinning the stand to reduce the fuel load. Keep pine needles from accumulating on roofs or in gutters, particularly during high fire season. Gutter guards may make this easier to do.

Blue Gum Eucalyptus

Blue gum eucalyptus *(Eucalyptus globules, myrtaccae)* is an Australian import planted in the mid-nineteenth century as a windbreak and in anticipation of timber production. It burns very hot, but has to be cured several months before using it as a fuel. It was intended for use as railroad ties and support timbers in mines but couldn't be worked because it would split. In Peru and Ecuador it's harvested for cooking fires, supports for adobe buildings, and flooring.

This very fast growing hardwood thrives in California but has negative effects on fish and wildlife and shades out other more desirable plants. Furthermore, it is a very tall tree subject to large limb failure that can block roads and destroy buildings. Living downwind or downhill from a towering eucalyptus places you and your home at great risk, plus you are liable if your tree damages a neighbor's property.

These trees are a notorious fire hazard. The aromatic oils in the leaves ignite easily, more so when they have dried out, and an accumulation of dead leaves, bark, and branches leads to a highly flammable fuel load that can exceed thirteen tons per acre. Fire spreads rapidly from the litter on the ground up the loose bark and into the crown, producing firebrands that can spread it for miles ahead of the fire front. Once a fire reaches the crowns of very tall trees, firefighters can not control it.

Eucalyptus is killed back by freezing, leaving a mass of dead wood susceptible to fire. The big freeze preceding the Oakland Firestorm of 1991 contributed to that fire as the surviving roots produced trees with multiple sprouts that were more prone to ignition than the original single-trunk trees.

Another variety, red gum eucalyptus, is frequently used in landscaping along roadways, including the Highway 24 corridor through the Oakland Hills. These trees are being killed off by an Australian insect, the lerp psillid, identifiable by one millimeter clamshell-like encrustations on the leaves. These dead trees are creating a widespread fire hazard.

1. Eradication

This is the most cost-effective strategy. First of all, don't plant them. Second, get 'em while they're small. Third, prevent re-sprouting.

It is imperative to paint the cambrian layer just within the bark of the cut stumps immediately with Garlon. Spraying them with Roundup can also work, but it can spread into the roots of nearby plants. Repeated cutting of sprouts as they appear may be effective over time but is labor intensive.

Disposal of the cut wood is a problem. It does not decompose noticeably over a dozen or more years, nor is there an identifiable market for it as fuel or flooring. It can burn hotter than a fireplace can handle and start the fire you were trying to prevent. Cutting eucalyptus without follow-up may well create a worse, multiple-trunk hazard as it sprouts voraciously.

Tall thin trees near houses are trickier to remove than heavier ones because they are easily blown the wrong direction by the wind. A crane may be required for control, costing $200 to $300 per tree. Larger trees may cost $1,000 to remove.

On steep slopes that are prone to erosion, one strategy is to prune trees to a height of 10 to 15 feet, cutting them back annually. This preserves the root system while giving more desirable trees a chance to get established. You can take advantage of the durability of cut logs by using them as roadside curbs or low retaining walls to control erosion.

2. Maintenance

Unfortunately, annual maintenance of large stands is very

laborious and expensive. You can reduce the fire ladder by pruning and thinning, removing large branches that could block a road or fall on a building.

The reduction of dead wood and litter will improve conditions for native plant growth. You can also remove smaller trees to reduce fuel ladders. Very large trees free of litter are a lesser hazard than a second-growth multiple-trunk tree.

French, Scotch and Spanish Broom

French broom *(Genistamonspessulana)*, Scotch broom *(Cytisusscoparius)* and Spanish broom *(Spartiumjunceum)* are non-native shrubs with beautiful yellow flowers. They thrive on disturbed slopes in fog-prone areas with sunny exposures. French and Scotch broom have small half-inch long yellow flowers and small light green to grey-green leaves. The less common Spanish broom has reed-like leaves and gorgeous one-inch bright yellow wax-like flowers. It grows faster and dies back faster. Hazards and management are the same for each.

1. Why Broom Is Such a Problem

Broom grows rapidly to 15 feet in height and six feet in width. Once it gains a foothold it is very prolific because mature plants can produce thousands of seeds annually. It grows up to 30 inches a year, quickly towering over most native vegetation and shading it out. Its dense growth can displace 75 percent of native plants. Within 20 years it can produce an impenetrable thicket displacing all plants except tall trees, driving out the birds and animals that depend on the native plants. The end result is an extremely high volume of flammable biomass.

Short-lived, fast-growing, and inches apart from one another, broom can generate a massive amount of kindling and grow tall enough to transmit fire into the crowns of trees. It grows in height for six to eight years, enters a period during which the ratio of woody to green material increases, and then dies. It becomes top-heavy and falls into great tangles. New seedlings grow straight up through the snarl, creating an even more complex mosaic of tinder. If a fire occurs, broom reseeds with a vengeance.

As if this were not bad enough, broom produces an oily substance that even deer and goats avoid. With no local source of natural control, an ideal climate, and a landscape under continuous onslaught by human "progress," broom is in weed heaven. A member of the pea family, it fixes nitrogen on its roots. It eventually creates an overly nitrogen-rich soil that encourages non-native grasses and weeds, which act as flash fuels.

Broom is overrunning the California coastal counties with disastrous effects on native plants and wildlife. Scotch broom is particularly bad in Point Reyes and Big Sur. A Portuguese variant has overtaken the foothills to the Andes in South America

2. Eradication

Eradication of broom requires obsessive long-term maintenance and follow up because of the substantial seed load that remains viable for years.

Your first goal should be to remove large plants, thus reducing biomass and preventing further contribution to the seed load. This is best done in spring before seeds mature. A weed wrench or pick axe can be used during the rainy season where disturbing the slope is not an issue, however, this is not advisable on a steep slope. Alternatively, if plants are over an inch in diameter, you can cut them off about 6" above the ground with a chainsaw or pruning saw. Since stems less than an inch in diameter tend to jam a chain saw, a pruning saw or loppers is preferable. Cut part way through the stem, then twist the tool and strip the bark down. Machetes don't work. Mowing and goats make things worse.

Spray or paint the raw stump immediately with concentrated Roundup or Rodeo before it seals. Failure to spray the stump will result in several stems growing from the cut trunk like a candelabra that can grow three feet in a single year and require multiple repeat cuts the next time around. If cut flush with the ground the plant has to be dug up laboriously by its roots, as the stems can't be cut.

On steep slopes it is easier and safer to work from the bottom up, leaning into the hill, using the cut stumps for a foothold, and throwing the cuttings below you as you go. It is important to be sure to spray each cut stump with Roundup because the stumps will soon rot and you may not be able to safely access the steep slope again.

Leaving the cut brush out for a week or two before removal allows the small leaves to fall off and dry up, reducing the volume to be removed. Disposing of this cut vegetation is time consuming and expensive, but you only have to do this after the first cut if you follow these suggestions.

3. Maintenance

Once the big plants are removed, you have to do regular maintenance or you will have wasted your time. This gets easier each year since there is no need to haul the cuttings to the roadside and have them carted away, or to create separated decomposition piles. Medium plants—up to an inch in diameter—can be pulled out by hand when the ground is wet, and their yellow flowers make them easy to identify. These cuttings are usually small enough that they can be left on the ground in separated piles. Seedlings can also be pulled at the same time, but the numbers may be staggering. You can use a pruning saw to rake them up by the roots with one hand while pulling with the other. It is easier to pull the surviving plants when they are a little larger and many of the seedlings have failed.

Allow no bloomin' broom to survive! It is crucial to pull all flowering broom so as to prevent new seed formation, diminishing the seed load each successive year. In large areas you need to patrol during the flowering season to spot volunteers that might infest an entirely new area. Encourage trees such as bay laurels that shade out the broom, which requires sun to thrive. There is often a surge of new seedlings after a heavy rain.

On steep slopes it is important to eradicate large plants on the first try, while one has a foothold on the cut stem below to reach the plant above. Subsequent maintenance may require ropes. When searching for resurgent broom on steep slopes, you can keep your hands free by putting roundup in a flat spray bottle like those used for Windex and tuck it inside your shirt. A Stihl pruning saw can be kept in a leather sheath attached to your belt, while you carry loppers in one hand. Be sure your tools are sharp. On the steepest slopes maintain contact with the slope with as many parts of your body as possible in case you slide feet first down the hill.

4. A Few Words about Roundup

The amount you need to use is quite minimal when squirted directly on the cut stems of larger plants not removable by other means. Most re-growth can be pulled out by hand during the wet season. After the first cutting, once the bulk of the plants is removed, very little herbicide will be needed, and less each year. At HHV where broom infestation has been extreme, a half gallon has lasted nearly 10 years. This is a far cry from the use of Roundup on agricultural crops by aerial spraying. The use of Roundup is legal on private lands but still extremely limited on Oakland city-owned properties. The grand jury in Marin County recommended that Roundup be used to help eradicate the massive growths of scotch broom present throughout the area because of their high fire hazard.

Pampas Grass

Pampas grass *(Cortaderia)* is a fast growing evergreen giant. It is an attractive plant with beautiful long silken fronds several feet in length. Over time it builds up a mass of dead material at its center. The dried fronds catch fire and act like torches, spreading fire to surrounding areas. Once the root ball catches fire it smolders and perpetuates the fire. Pampas grass is an indicator of an underlying water source that may warn of a landslide risk. It can form dense masses of plants that are difficult to remove. It has invaded the cliffs of Big Sur, where it is impossible to eradicate.

Management of pampas grass involves cutting the fronds in summer and bagging them headfirst in a large trash bag to prevent the spread of seeds during removal. After winter rains have saturated the ground, seedlings and smaller plants can be pickaxed with relative ease.

Large plants can also be pickaxed, but this is hard work. Alternatively, you can use a pruning saw, loppers or even a chain saw to cut to the base of the plant, which can then be sprayed directly with Roundup. This is best done at the same time you remove the fronds. Aim directly at the cut frond end and at the remaining leaves. Later the dead mass will be easier to remove and any sprouts can be cut and resprayed. When dug up, allow root balls to dry out, reducing their mass before carrying them away.

Appendix C—Maximizing Dumpster Use

Provided by local waste management districts, dumpsters are widely used for the removal and recycling of flammable vegetation in vegetation management programs. The Oakland Wildfire Prevention District was offered free dumpsters to support homeowners who grouped together to reduce flammable vegetation in a neighborhood. This provided a significant saving to homeowners as the cost of removing cut vegetation can easily exceed the cost of cutting it.

Here are some tips to make the most efficient use of a dumpster.

1. Be very clear about where the dumpster is to be placed. Providing a map to the waste management company isn't enough. Mark the exact site clearly with orange cones and staked cardboard signs. It's no fun hauling cut vegetation an extra 30 feet.

2. Consider posting a sign that says something like:

FIRE PREVENTION
WORKDAY HERE
SATURDAY

3. Such a sign could be reused any Saturday. It facilitates getting the dumpster placed in the right location and at the same time advertises the workday.

4. You are responsible for what goes into the dumpster, so minimize the time the dumpster is onsite to reduce the chances of passersby using it for their personal trash. Dumpsters aren't delivered or picked up on weekends.

5. Cut some vegetation before the dumpster is delivered

and have it ready to load quickly once the dumpster arrives. Consider cutting vegetation a week or two before to give it time to dry out, reducing the weight and volume. This is especially true for French broom because its leaves will dry up and drop off.

6. It helps greatly if someone can go into the dumpster with a chainsaw to cut up the debris and compact it, substantially increasing the amount you can get into the dumpster. At a minimum, use loppers to cut up branches.

7. Another option is to use a shredder. These are rentable but dangerous. Most tree services can provide them with an operator.

8. Cover the dumpster with a tarp to prevent it from being used for trash.

The author at work pulling invasive annual grasses from a robust naturally occurring stand of California fescue, a native bunch grass whose deep roots help stabilize the soil on this steep 45 degree slope.